# Jane Doe Overdose

## An Addiction Story

drliam16@gmail.com
www.re4vitality.com

Facebook: @rejuvme , @janedoeoverdose

ISBN-13:978-1540688484.   ISBN-10: 1540688488

Author: Dr. Liam Briones

Script consultants: Sean Moran and Don Blesdoe

Layout & Design

Dr. Liam

Cover photo Dr. Liam
(Cleveland Skyline from a high rise building on a foggy day-
April 2015, Cleveland, OH)

Table of Contents

**51**

## DEDICATION:

This book is dedicated to the relatives of those lost to heroin overdose. I feel your pain and I join you in a campaign to improve the lives of those currently suffering from opiate addiction. There is great need to shift efforts into healing not persecuting and into improving outcomes from rehabilitation centers and correctional centers rather than treating violence with more violence.

In good health,

Dr. Briones MD, MBA, FCCP, FSCCM, FAASM, FA4M, FICT, P.Sc.D

# PROLOGUE

*— Cleveland, Ohio — 1990*

A white, non-descript van screeched to a halt under an ominous Cleveland bridge underpass. The night was chilly and small fires in adapted coffee can pits could be seen from the dirt road leading as close to the underpass as they could maneuver.

"We can find them here," Chad intoned.

Grace nervously clutched a well-worn backpack. This was her first evening out with the teen rescue outreach, so her apprehensiveness was normal, in fact, expected.

Night Visitors was in its tenth year of operation, surviving on a minimal budget funded by local area churches. The non- denominational group was a lifeline for runaway teenagers, dozens of them. It operated from a donated basement space primarily used for storage and preparation of food.

"Grace, get the sandwiches out of your bag so they will know we are here to help. They're going to be scared, cold and hungry. It's essential to assure them we mean no harm," he said calmly.

Grace fumbled with the pack and pulled out peanut butter sandwiches, fruit and beverages, recently expired, but still good for their purpose. Grace had also bought some candy bars with her own money as an additional contribution.

Her parents had hoped for a degree in something more substantial than social studies, but that's where her heart was. Even from a young age, she was always socially conscious, running Kool-Aid stands benefiting local food pantries. She had earned the nickname "Sister Grace," which irritated her immensely. She felt that one didn't have to have a religious vocation to care for their fellow man. In fact, it had nothing to do with religion, it had to do with human compassion and empathy.

The group navigated through discarded debris beneath the underpass. Grace slipped a few times, nearly cutting herself on a broken bottle.

"Careful, Grace, watch the glass," a smile crossed his face, "And don't wear good shoes when you're out here."

He continued to lead the way; his flashlight played around in the darkness. Soon there was movement to their left, up under the bridge by the fires.

"We have some food for you and blankets if you need them," he called out calmly. Slowly, a small group of shrouded figures approached cautiously.

Grace's hand shook as she held out a sandwich, snatched from her by a dirty hand.

"Thank you," a girl said.

Miranda Anders hadn't eaten in days. The strung-out young girl shivered as she devoured the sandwich, dropping the inedible plastic wrap into the pocket of a dirty tattered jean jacket. Grace fumbled to get a drink opened before it was snatched from her.
Chad proceeded with caution.

"So, what's your name?" he gently asked.

"You have anything else to eat? It's been a while," she asked politely.

Grace handed her an apple from home that she brought for herself.

"Fruit? I don't eat that," Miranda said, "But Carmen will."

Grace fumbled for a candy bar which Miranda grabbed and slipped back into the darkness.

"We have blankets if you need it," Chad called to her. No answer.

As Chad and Grace drove to their next location, he didn't say a word as Grace cried quietly to herself. They had all cried the first time. It was almost a rite of passage. Chad himself almost never came back after his first time, the experience almost broke his heart. He too had parents who had hoped for a doctor or a lawyer but were eventually proud of his choice.

"I'm going to have to watch you carefully," he whispered to Grace.

"And why is that?" she

asked. "Because you
care too much." "And
you don't?"

He answered quickly, "Of course I do, but meas-
uredly. I don't want you to burn out."

"Oh, I won't," she smiled back, "I plan on being
around for a long time."

"I hope so."

Thank God she didn't become a nun.

# CHAPTER 1

*— Cleveland, Ohio — 2010*

Nurse Reyes grabbed her coffee from the car as she parked on the eighth-floor structure at St. Vincent Charity Hospital. She dropped her keys in the slush as she sipped from the McDonald's cup.

"Son of a bitch, stone cold," she muttered as she tossed the entire cup beside the car. She trudged toward the elevator, giving the finger to the "DO NOT LITTER" sign posted on the wall. As she reached the elevator, a hand-scrawled sign read "Out of Order. Use stairs."

"Really, instead of just jumping?" she muttered as she took the stairs.

Despite it all, Cheskka Reyes loved her job in the St. Vincent E.R. But this was one of her most hated days — Friday.

Having not even punched in yet, and shit had already started. Firstly, it's not a day shift, but night, it was five below zero and it was Friday the 13th to boot.

"At least I get to work with my boys." The "boys" were her favorite E.R. team.

Washington Carver Johnson — what were his parents thinking — possibly one of the hottest black men on the planet and everyone knew that but him. Sweet and vulnerable, which meant a lifetime of heartbreak. Women eat men like him for lunch, something she was not proud of. She had thought that maybe there should be something between them, but she had tried dating in-house once before and it turned out to be a bad episode of "General Hospital." She shuddered at the memory.

Dr. Patrick Edwards was the on-call physician. Interestingly enough, he was both a physician and a Roman Catholic priest. No kidding. A long story short, Patrick married his high school sweetheart, had two boys and climbed the hospital ladder quickly due to his diligence and work ethic. Tragically, his wife died of pancreatic cancer at forty-one. Devastated at the sudden loss he took solace in his faith. Knowing there would never be another woman like Genevieve and knowing he would never remarry, he became a priest. This sometimes happens with widowers entering the seminary as second generation candidates.

Patrick continued life as a parent to Terrance and Séan, as Dr. Edwards and now as Father Edwards. The hospital now had an in- house chaplain and doctor rolled into one. He was also a dead ringer for Richard Gere.

Cheskka loved seeing the reaction of a new nurse batting her flirtatious eyes at him for nothing.

"Oh, you didn't know? He's a priest," she delivered with precision.

"Hello, princess," smiled Alvin, the E.R. dispatcher, "You're just in time. We have a nineteen-year-old female, right eye superglued shut, a two-year-old male with a football injury —"

"Two… with a football injury?" she interjected. "Dos," as he held up two fingers.

"Lovely parents," she muttered.

"And a possible poisoning. You'll love this one, Jatrophia Curcas," he smiled.

"Is she a drag queen?"

He howled, "No, it's the poison, a flowering plant from the tropics with some very good parts and some very bad parts. Twenty-seven-year-old male ingested the bad parts."

"Did he get it at Wealthy Living?"

Again, through laughter, "No, apparently he's a missionary from Brazil."

"I hope he looks like Benny Feihaber." Alvin stared at her blankly.

"Hottie soccer player? Okay, you're one of those."

Nodding his head, "No football, no baseball, no basketball —" She walked away, "Yes, I know the balls you like to handle." "Sexual harassment, Missy," he joked.

"Harassment, my ass."

A loud voice pierced the busy E.R. and Alvin immediately planted himself in front of the squawk box, pen in one hand, Dunkin Donut in the other.

The box crackled, "Life Care 24 ... en route with an unresponsive female mid-thirties ... found half-dressed behind a dumpster in a mountain of snow ... no obvious signs of assault ... smells strongly of alcohol ... needle stuck in her arm. No response to Narcan ... patient is breathing and has a pulse ... BP 90/60 ...

HR 55 ... RR 16 ... pulse OX unable due to cold fingers ... IV 2 started with fluid boluses initiated ... ETA five minutes."

Alvin searched for the team working in Bay 4 with the two-year-old. He motioned Nurse Cheskka over.

"Alvin?"

"Cheskka, we got an icicle on the way. Looks drug related. ETA in five."

Washington Carver looked up from the child, "And we're off."

Dr. Edwards paused and also looked up, "W.C., just keep him quiet." He turned to Cheskka, "Let's go."

They both ran to meet the ambulance as it arrived at the entrance. EMTs Carlos and Menendez wheeled in the unresponsive patient strapped to the gurney.

"Bay number?" Dr. Edwards looked to Alvin. "Two."

They whisked her into the bay and routinely transferred her to the exam table.

Jane Doe was pale, white, severely cold and rigid. Her robot-like movement was also in slow motion with labored breathing. The patient was medicated to paralyze her muscles, allowing the team to insert a tube down her throat. The patient was warmed with saline in the traditional manner for resuscitation of a hypothermia victim.

Dr. Edwards was able to raise her temperature from 27°C (81°F) to 28°C (82°F). On further examination, it was discovered she had an alcohol level of 400 and was the reason the Narcan did not work.

In terms of hypothermia, her case was severe, and death was imminent.

Dr. Edwards motioned Cheskka out of the bay.

"She's not a Jane Doe," he quietly stated, "Unfortunately, I know her well."

Nurse Carlson interrupted them both, "Doctor,

we need you to change hats. The poisoned patient is critical and is asking for a priest."

He turns to Cheskka, "I'll brief you later on Miranda."

He reached into his pocket to retrieve the purple stole and placed it around his neck for the Anointing of the Sick sacrament. It was the same ritual and different name for the one formerly known as Last Rites. He didn't know why it had changed and always felt Last Rites was a more fitting name. Even as a young boy, he giggled at learning the Latin term "Extreme Unction." Every Catholic house had the magic cross on the wall. It could be taken down, slit open to reveal two small candles and a glass vial for Holy Water. The whole contraption functioned as a mini altar.

Cheskka and W.C. continued to monitor Miranda who began to shiver just barely. Her skin was flushed and muscles remained rigid, but the slight shiver was a positive sign. Despite her "frozen stiff" status, Cheskka could see that she was once a beauty with blonde hair and green eyes.

"Looks like she'll pull through," W.C. commented.

"Again. Dr. Edwards said she's been here many times before.

Apparently, our Jane Doe has a name," Cheskka recounted.

Dr. Edwards had slipped back into the room quietly with a well- worn file in hand.

He motioned to the patient on the gurney.

"This is Miranda Anders," he said as he approached the patient and handed the file to Cheskka, who flipped through its pages.

"How is the missionary guy?" W.C. whispered.

"Mr. Romero was called at 1:35 AM. I have to do some research on that particular poison. Sadly, it's extremely toxic," Dr. Edwards said, "Let's just keep an eye on Miranda here."

W.C. adjusted the equipment and left the bay.

"Cheskka, do me a favor. Find out if the EMTs used a Res-Q-Air machine en route. They did something to her because from the looks of this, we should have lost her. Very impressive," he nodded.

"I see from her chart," Cheskka noted, "We've almost lost her several times. Miranda Anders, 1996, 22 years of age, presented to the E.R. with a heroin overdose after having been dumped from a car."

"Yes, apparently her dealer noticed the fix was going south, didn't want to be caught with a dead body and pushed her out of the vehicle without stopping."

She continued reading the chart.

"Year 2005, now 31, the patient was admitted, allegedly raped due to abrasions covering the torso, upper arms and thighs. They were particularly prominent around the neck, indicating her attacker had choked her at some point during penetration. As you continue, you'll notice Miranda had been admitted half a dozen times with abdominal pain or migraine headaches, usual ploys by the addicted in seeking narcotics. If you can't get them on the street, come visit your friendly E.R. Luckily, we could utilize the database to check if she was listed."

The shift had been long, but with the sunrise came time to punch out. Cheskka and W.C. planned to catch breakfast at the corner diner. As she left, she checked in with Dr. Edwards, still in his office making chart notes.

"Hey, time to go home."

"I'm going to stick around for a bit and see if we can get Miranda into a rehab program," he stated matter-of-factly.

"Good luck with that. Do you want something from the diner?" "No, I'll get something from the cafeteria."

Cheskka shook her head, "And end up with the Jatrophia Curcas."

"Ah!" his face lit up, "I knew I was forgetting something. I need to look that little bugger up."

She smiled to herself as she closed his door.

Against her better judgment, she invited W.C. to her house for breakfast.

Girl, you never learn.

# CHAPTER 2

*— Ancient History — 1985*

Miranda had a secret.

Virginia and Harry Anders had a storybook life. Having been the typical high school sweethearts, it surprised no one when they married right out of high school. No college for either, Harry and his identical twin, Ted, had turned an inherited garage into a multi-million dollar truck rental company. If one had to move 50 or 5,000 miles, customers used an Anders Rental truck, dollies, boxes and expensive paraphernalia. Recently, the brothers had been exploring the opportunity for an out of the country moving venture. You want to live in Australia? Call us and we'll set it up for you.

Virginia, a blonde buxom beauty, divided her time between her husband, the gym and trying to spend each and every last penny he had. Meticulous about her looks, she had a small addiction to plastic surgery. Nothing major, just minor nips and tucks that resulted in her being full of mercury amalgams which she would pass on in utero to her daughter.

But.

Virginia also had a secret.

While Harry relished his latest passion, off-trail skiing in the Alps, Virginia delved into her biggest passion, actually a vice.

Mommy was a sex addict. Starting with Sven, her stair-step instructor, moving on to Mario, the co-owner of the gym, then to the gardener and to the carpenter, who banged more than just the wood. Her latest conquest, the lawn boy, was actually the gardener's son, fifteen and hung. Shame, shame, shame. Only there was no shame for Virginia, just another notch on her imaginary bedpost.

Harry, an adrenaline junkie, had moved from sports cars sponsored by the Anders Team to para-gliding. His latest addiction was a return to a sport of his youth. Back then, it was a local ski slope with one T-bar in someone's backyard in Vermont and now it was designer skis, boots and being dropped from a helicopter on the peak of a mountain in the Alps. His brother Ted had often accompanied him in the past, but in recent years he too found a new passion.

Harry's wife, Virginia.

And their young daughter, Miranda.

The Technicolor storybook life had a seedy black and white side, as dark as midnight. It started innocently, as revolting as it is to   use that word to describe a man's affair with his brother's wife.

Harry, off skiing, poor Virginia left alone with only money to keep her company, what was a guy to do? In Ted's twisted mind, he was doing his brother favor, keeping the family together. Otherwise, she would run off with the gardener, the carpenter or the under-aged boy she was doing, and sometimes a threesome with the kid's father. Oh yes, he knew of every single last conquest. In fact, it made him want her more and gave him quite the bargaining chip.

Not really a chip, but blackmail.

Ted had no moral compass being a deviant sociopath. No conscience for the feelings of others, he had been bleeding the company of money for years and was accomplished at covering his tracks. But it was easy since his brother and partner was seldom around. As for Virginia, an abortion here and there was her problem.

Harry continued to be absent and Ted took advantage of the situation. As often happens with social deviants who lust for power and dominance, Ted's attention grew toward dalliances other than Virginia.

Miranda, his niece.

The pampered life of an only-child raised with affluent parents often turns out well, but not for this family. As Virginia and Ted's relationship continued, a new one blossomed.

Virginia, no dumb blonde, saw it, hated it and had

no choice in the matter. Ted had the goods on her, the times, the places, the men. He hands were tied or in this case, she had to keep her mouth shut.

She found solace first in the bottle and then moved on to prescription drugs. Oxycodone was her first choice. Unbeknownst to her, she had set up a blueprint for her daughter to also cope with the sexual abuse that continued for five years.

By the time Miranda had reached sixteen, she was an alcoholic, a drug abuser, the recipient of one abortion, but luckily no longer molested by her uncle.

Sometimes in life, bad things happen to good people. Less often, the planets line up perfectly, called karma, and the bad people get what they deserve.

After a long night of drinking and an extended session of especially rough sex with Virginia, Ted found himself angry and exhausted on his way home. That bitch had suggested a three-way with some other guy.

"What the fuck was she thinking?" he muttered out loud to himself as he pounded the steering wheel.

"That's fine for her, but I don't want another dude in the same bed, it's just sick."

As he sped along in his Porsche 911, complete with leather interior and power steering, Ted fumbled to reach a cassette tape to get himself out of the funk he was in. As he bent to reach the tape off the floor, he veered into the oncoming lane of U.S. Highway 20.

Ted was killed instantly in a head-on collision with an eighteen wheeler, and as karma would have it, the truck was one of the Anders fleet.

The Gods had smiled on Miranda.

"You fool around with little girls, you lose your head." Literally.

Virginia, on the other hand, was despondent. Honestly feeling that Ted was more of a husband to her than Harry, she pulled and "Valley of the Dolls" and committed suicide by overdosing on vodka and pills.

Either way, Miranda was free of both of them.

# CHAPTER 3

*— Luke — 1988*

The world of a fourteen-year-old is often filled with puppy dogs, princesses in pink and the adoration of John Depp, the reigning teen idol, often displayed in a 3x5 posters covering the wall. Such was not the case for Miranda, due to years of abuse by her father's twin, her mother's promiscuity, drug abuse and alcoholism.

So much for Santa and the Easter bunny.

Any hopes for a normal childhood had long been shattered.

To escape the reality of her world, Miranda had developed a keen sense of art. Her sketches were dark, foreboding and haunting and found no better muse for her work than the bus station. Armed with a drawing pad and a pocketful of #2 pencils, she sat for hours, sketching away. More often than not, she drew the stares of passengers in the terminal, wondering to themselves why a fourteen-year-old girl was alone at midnight.

She ignored them.

She ignored everybody, except for this one boy. He was always there. Sometimes dirty, sometimes not. Sometimes eating, sometimes not. But always staring.

Luke, as she would come to find out, was a runaway, having left home in the Midwest for no reason other than to get away from religious zealots posing as parents. He lived hand-to-mouth, earning what little money he had by turning tricks, with women or men.

He didn't care.

They were just a meal.

At first, it was an innocent game. His stares from bench to bench, across a myriad of passengers on the way to anywhere else, never phased her. She just continued to draw. To her amusement, in his subtle way, Luke would pose for her. Nothing overt, maybe a glance, maybe a repositioning of his hand, requiring her to turn the page and start over. She hated erasing.

One day he crossed the great divide and sat next to her. "Let me see," Luke whispered.

"That's what they all say," she said provocatively without looking up from her pad.

"That's dirty."

"It's a dirty world."

Her use of that word spoke volumes. Educated, lonely and already soured on life, it was love at first sight.

"Luke," he said as he extended his hand.

"Miranda," she answered as she continued to draw. He peeked down at the sketch, "Looks just like me." "You're sad."

"So are you."

Their fate was sealed. For the next year, Miranda and Luke were inseparable. They would sit side by side and he would recount his liaisons to her while she drew. He never spoke of his past, only the present, and god forbid, nothing of the future. It's as if he knew there was no future for him.

"So, the guy was married?" she asked.

"I guess so. He had a ring," he stated matter-of-factly, "Just a simple blow and go."

"I hate those," she muttered. "Your uncle?"

"Who else."

"I'm really not into dudes," he said, "But there's not a lot of women looking to pay for it with an eighteen-year-old boy."

"Their loss."

Silence.

He ate. She drew.

"Was it weird for you?" he finally asked. She finally looked up.

"What aspect of my life are you referring to?" she asked with a smirk.

"Sex with your father's twin brother ... I mean ... Is it like having sex with your father himself?"

"It's been so long; I try not to think of that." "Did your mother know?" he asked.

She just stared vacantly into space.

Several months later, Miranda was pregnant with their child, along with another gift Luke had shared with her.

He had penchant for smack, which unfortunately wasn't cheap.

That's where Miranda came in.

Along with her artistic ability, she was an excellent forger, this time to the tune of five thousand dollars. Harry would never notice.

Hell, he hardly noticed her.

With her newfound fortune, she packed a small bag to begin a new life with Luke. Having the wherewithal to realize her chances of having a crack baby was high, they decided on a first trimester abortion, being within the first twelve weeks of her pregnancy, it was easily accomplished with a forged letter from her father. Hand in hand, they sat in the waiting room office of the Eighth Street Women's Clinic.

The two were a Norman Rockwell painting, had Mr. Rockwell been a twisted artist with a warped view of Romeo & Juliet. It did not go unnoticed by the other patients that this couple was both very young and equally strung out. It was love in some sense of the word, albeit on the dark side of the spectrum. The only drawback with an abortion was the loss of a pregnant young girl begging for money outside Starbucks. Luke and Miranda both realized this would have been a financial bonanza since they had blown through the $5,000 on premium heroin, Belvedere vodka and Taco Bell.

Their usual procurement for funds would dry up and the jewelry and rings from her dead mother were among the first to go.

They had celebrated in style, strung out at Chez Pierre, a very upscale French restaurant and paid for the bill in the old fashioned dine-and-dash way. It was their favorite because it had a back entrance.

Daddy now realized his fifteen-year-old teenage daughter had run away with his money and was nowhere to be found. He sold his company to Penske for an unprecedented $1 billion dollars, closed the house and returned to the world of Scotch, skis and slopes.

Thus, the money train ended and Romeo & Juliet were on their own.

After the procedure, Miranda and Luke returned to their room at the No-Tell Motel. As atypical as this relationship was, it truly was love. Luke, a blond haired, blue eyed giant of a boy was Miranda's protector. Instead of turning her out to trick for money, that was his job as the provider.

It was an old-fashioned relationship.

Daddy earned the money and mommy stayed home, only in this case, mommy wasn't pregnant anymore.

With his looks, Luke had no problems earning a Benjamin per trick. His best marks were the men from the top of The Hill. It was amazing to him how a plethora of married senators needed to be dominated. Luke was young, willing and readily available.

He was equipped for the job with the tools of the trade: a new flip-phone (a gift from one of his regulars) and an expensive suit and tie worn only for the occasion (the best hotels prefer them).

The clincher was
personal. He was
hung like a horse.

A stolen prescription for antibiotics was last in his arsenal, since syphilis and gonorrhea occurred often.

An occupational hazard.

Miranda and Luke existed in their vagabond lifestyle for nearly two years until Luke was picked up and jailed for grand larceny.

An expensive bracelet he had pilfered from Tiffany's as a birthday gift for his Juliet, was his ticket to the graybar hotel.

With Luke incarcerated, the situation worsened and Miranda found herself in an encampment of homeless living under the Veterans Memorial Bridge. No longer protected by her tainted knight in shining armor, she panhandled as best she could and often reverted to the "pregnancy plea," a well-placed pillow under her dress. Had she planned ahead, he could have had an actual babe-in-arms, always a heartbreaker and an easy buck.

# CHAPTER 4

*— Grace — 1990*

"Hola, Chiquita," Carmen whispered as she shook Miranda, "Dos people are here with food, hungry?"

The "residents" of the encampment under this side of the Veterans Memorial Bridge were couple of dozen, both men and women, middle-aged down to teenaged runaways. Miranda was one of the youngest and less seasoned. Carmen had lived here with her husband until he passed away. From her broken English, she had shared with Miranda their story. Illegals from Cuba, they had actually owned and ran a small Cuban eatery, very popular in Cleveland. One day, immigration raided the restaurant for undocumented workers and Carmen and Rodrigo barely escaped deportation, and lived on the streets ever since.

Carmen, alone now, had adopted Miranda and kept the men at bay with a fierce temper and a big knife. She knew from her years on the street how vulnerable youth was, both female and male. A couple of years previously one of the bridge family, Kurt, a runaway from Mount Cory was brutally raped and beaten not far from here. Carmen blamed herself and became "Mom" to the kids in the camp.

Miranda hurried to get up and get the food. She couldn't remember if she had eaten yesterday or not.

"I get one for you too, Carmen," she whispered.

Through the softness of her gaze, Miranda knew she too was hungry, but too proud to take a hand-out.

She scurried down toward the people emerging from the van.

Grace's hand shook as she held out a sandwich, snatched from her by a dirty hand.

"So, what's your name?" he gently asked.

"Nobody's business. You got anything else to eat, it's been a while," she stated, "And there are others."

Grace handed her an apple.

"Fruit? I don't eat that," Miranda said, "But Carmen will." "Good, good," Grace commented. She then reached into her bag for an extra sandwich and a chocolate bar, not knowing if it was against the rules.

"Here's a sandwich for Carmen, candy for you," Grace whispered.

Miranda looked up to the face connected to the hand. She couldn't explain it, but there was connection there.

The woman was ... different. Not odd or weird, just different. Miranda didn't know then the role Grace would play in her life.

"We'll be here again tomorrow about this time," Grace said softly, "Do you need anything else?"

Without hesitation, Miranda replied,

"Soap." Grace smiled, "That, I can do."

Grace and Miranda's relationship continued under the bridge for a year. Grace often wondered how her "bridge people" survived the weather through the seasons.

One day it all changed. She arrived at the usual time, sandwiches in hand, but no Miranda.

She had disappeared.

# CHAPTER 5

*— Another Man — 1993*

Miranda loathed begging or stealing, but she had to survive. She had perfected the "fall and search" method Luke had introduced to her when they were together. The scenario was a fancy restaurant, ladies who lunch with a few too many vodka stingers and an innocent girl who happened to trip near their table. As she struggled to get up, she had quickly rifled through their purses on the floor and grabbed a wallet or two.

Miranda kept herself neat and clean by bathing in the Macy's bottom floor ladies' room that had sparse foot traffic. Despite the drug use, she was still attractive at nineteen. Blonde haired, blue- eyed with a petite figure, her smile was still amazingly brilliant. She was dressed in her working wardrobe, a teal blue dress kept neat and clean in her cardboard enclosure under the bridge.

Today's target, Chez L'Orange, a busy upscale establishment was the perfect mark for her heist.

Now for the OSCAR award winning performance.

Miranda approached the hostess coyly, requesting a table for one. As she passed by a table of four middle-aged women, she tripped. With a heavy dose of moaning, she feigned injury causing the hostess to panic and created confusion. As people ran to assist, the ladies stood back, Miranda quickly searched for the nearest handbag to pilfer the wallet.

After leaving the restaurant, she followed her one, major rule. Cash pocketed and the credit card must be used with a sixty minute limit. The card was then discarded immediately after wiping it down in a handy lady's room. Equipped with her list, she shopped precisely and efficiently within the time allotted and discarded the card and emptied wallet.

She always felt guilty for her actions.

As she blended with the downtown foot traffic, laden with her purchases, she paused to look at her reflection in the corner Starbucks window. Staring back at her was a handsome man in his late twenties.

Robert O'Sullivan, Sully to his friends, was mesmerized. Unlucky in love, he decided to take another chance. He immediately stood up from his coffee and muffin, and exited to assist the "fair young maiden" staring at her reflection in the window. Realizing no one would think of her in these terms, it was just part of his realm as the proud owner of the very successful "King Arthur's Medieval Dinner Theatre."

"Can I help you?" he said with a polar cap melting smile.

Flustered, she handed him a bag, forgetting momentarily she couldn't take him home under the bridge. The view was nice, but she hated the furniture, early shopping cart was never tasteful.

"Sure," she handed him a bag to carry.

That small gesture between them seemed to seal their fate.

For the next few weeks Miranda miraculously avoided the issue of where she actually lived. Blinded by love, Sully never pursued the matter. Within a month, she had moved in with him and they were married. Again, the issue of her lack of possessions never came up.

She simply explained it, "Let the past remain there. I want to focus on our future together."

That was good enough for him.

The storybook marriage mirrored one of the paintings of Lancelot and Guinevere hanging in the lobby of his medieval restaurant. All perfect, all loving and soon including the addition of a son. Sully had found true happiness with Miranda. She too had found a true love.

Except for her secret.

Heroin.

By an unbelievable chance encounter, Luke, released from prison, had reunited with Miranda. Perfect for them both, she could be the ideal wife and mother during the day, and addict at night.

Husband worked and wife played.

In order to hide her heroin use, she had snorted, but soon became bored with the moderate high it produced. She then resorted to shooting it painfully between her toes to hide the track marks from Sully.

Life was lived in this double identity for years.

Sully and Miranda welcomed their first child, Arthur, ten months after their wedding to the adoration of Sully's parents, her new found in-laws.

Sully's first marriage had ended in an annulment after petitioning the Church as to the sexual preference of his first wife, Valerie ... who had run off with Linda and presumably lived happily ever after. To the O'Sullivan's, the birth of a child was an indication of a perfect marriage.

Even Miranda's father, Harry, managed to meet his grandson and actually took a liking to the child. It was bittersweet for Miranda, since he was oblivious to the hell of her own childhood. To this point, he never knew of the molestation she suffered for years at the hands of his brother.

Soon, she would learn that CSA, child sexual abuse, is a term used to describe any illicit conduct between an adult and a child, ranging from voyeurism to actual rape. Statistically, 14% of women with a CSA history have some form of substance dependence, often it was both alcohol and drugs.

By a cruel twist of fate, the re-emergence of Luke into her life continued into her own personal tragedy with one huge difference, she now had money. Sully's restaurant had done so well that he  was about to open a second location in Washington, DC. This necessitated a considerable amount of travel on his part and with a nanny for Arthur, Miranda was free to play.

And play hard she did.

Through time served in prison, Luke had finessed his drug connections and with Miranda's husband's checkbook, they could score the finest and the purest highs.

Heroin, processed from morphine, naturally occurs in the seed pods of poppy plants. It is sold in a white or brown powder and is "cut" with sugar, starch or powdered milk. This drug can be injected, snorted or smoked. Leery of injection, Miranda had chosen to snorted her score, to Luke's dismay, who was injecting his.

"It's a much better high," Luke softly prompted her. She nodded in agreement, but protested.

"Tracks, Luke, tracks," as she pointed to her arm. "Your loss."

The mere fact Miranda balanced her life as Mrs. O'Sullivan with Miranda Anders was amazing. In Hollywood terms, it would have been a role any actress would have died to play.

All was about to change.

On July 14, 1996, Luke and Miranda had been partying in his one room walk-up above the Quicker Liquor store. As he gazed out the window at the buzzing, red and green flickering neon sign, the glow illuminated Miranda's face. He had finally convinced her to take the high road and shoot their score. As he watched her tighten the tourniquet, he realized she was horribly out of practice.

"Let me help you," he insisted.

"I can do it myself," she protested.

"You'll love it this way. You're gonna feel it in seconds."

He proceeded to load the syringe from the dirty spoon containing the liquefied score.

"Stop squirming!" he demanded.

A needle placed flat to the skin won't move and when inserted, goes straight down the vein and not across it. Unfortunately, this time the smack missed the vein and formed a heroin blister, which would take hours to be absorbed by the body.

"Ouch, that burns!" she shouted.

"That's because it didn't go into
the vein." "Fuck!"

The next evening after Miranda tucked her children in for the night, she instructed the nanny that she would be out doing "charity work" and hurried to Luke's hovel.

During the day, Luke had scored some pure Hell Dust. Miranda haphazardly parked her car around the corner, risking a citation, she hurried from the vehicle. "Screw the ticket," she thought, "I have a glove box full."

As she rushed around the corner nearly knocking into an elderly woman with a bag of groceries, she apologized and smirked as she looked up and noticed a huge poster in the liquor store window downstairs from Luke's apartment.

"Drugs = Death."

Without a lot of small talk, a peck on the cheek signaled the evening had begun, and Luke was ready.

"You'll love this stuff," he smiled through a slight daze, "I bought it just for you. I did some other stuff earlier."

She tossed her purse and coat onto the frayed Salvation Army couch, missing it and they landed on the sticky, splintered floor.

Once again the tourniquet was placed, the needle loaded and the fix was delivered directly into the vein in seconds.

Bingo.

The elusive high Miranda had never felt before flooded her body.

Neither had known the smack Miranda had used was cut with strychnine, a colorless bitter alkaloid which, when absorbed, results in muscular convulsions, eventually causing death through asphyxia.

An hour later and almost too late, Luke realized Miranda's high had slipped into a coma. The needle had also broken off in her arm and he struggled to remove the remaining piece of it.

"Shit, shit, shit!" he panicked.

Frantically, he searched and found Miranda's car keys, lifted   her up and staggered down the stairs to the sidewalk and searched for her car. Finding it around the corner, he maneuvered her into  the passenger seat and took off, nearly sideswiping another car as  he screeched down the street. A traffic ticket blocked his view. He turned on the wipers to reach for the ticket and tossed it into the street.

Minutes later, he spotted a blue hospital sign for St. Vincent and careened around the corner and to head toward Emergency.

Barely coming to a halt at the entrance, he struggled to reach across Miranda. Unfastening his seat belt, he stretched to open the passenger door to push her out of the car.

"Sorry babe, I can't risk going back to jail," he muttered as she hit the pavement with a thud.

He slammed the car door and pounded on the car horn to alert the staff inside.

# CHAPTER 6

*— St. Vincent — 1996*

Miranda's introduction to the E.R. at St. Vincent and Dr.

Patrick Edwards was under the worst of circumstances.

"Twenty-year-old Jane Doe found on the ground, apparent drug overdose, broken needle at right arm injection site," the nurse recited to the physician's assistant as they transferred her into an open E.R. bay.

"Get Doctor Edwards in here," the nurse insisted.

The patient was treated with Naloxone intravenously and luckily responded within five seconds, vomited her last meal all over the trauma bay and staff.

"Any identification?" Dr. Edwards

asked. "Nothing, Jane Doe," replied the nurse.

"Well, keep checking with the police to see if someone files a missing person's report matching our patient."

Days later, Sully indeed filed that report having returned from his D.C. trip. Ghostly white, he sat quietly in Dr. Edwards office.

"Her heroin addiction unfortunately has a long history and I suggest rehab immediately."

"I had no idea," Sully said quietly as if in Church. "Often times, family members never do."

"I've just been out of town so much," Sully blamed himself.

"It's not your fault, it's not even hers, she's an addict," it pained Dr. Edwards to say.

Dr. Edwards reached into his desk drawer to get a pamphlet and handed it to Mr. O'Sullivan.

"This is a pamphlet for Harmony House, an excellent rehab center here in town where she can get the help she needs." To emphasize his point, he continued, "And she needs it now."

As painful as it was for Sully to realize he had married a drug addict, he was in love with his wife enough to insist, despite her protestations, she go to rehab.

# CHAPTER 7

*— Harmony House — 1996*

In a traditional rehabilitation environment, the primary goal is to rehabilitate the patient with a program unshackling addiction to their particular nemesis — in Miranda's case, heroin. When one uses this drug regularly enough, the body adapts. Therefore, the need for more and stronger heroin ensues until the user's life and financial circumstances are destroyed.

Or the worst-case scenario, death.

In choosing a facility, there is an inpatient or an outpatient alternative, both Dr. Edwards and Sully felt that inpatient was the best choice for Miranda. The most common treatment time is the 30-day program, but for Miranda a 60-day program was initiated. Sully decided that since money was not a limiting factor, the longer program, with its higher rate of success, was better for Miranda's long-term prognosis.

Privacy and confidentiality were important to Sully since he was well-known in the business community, but Miranda's health was his utmost concern.

After intake, which included a physical exam and psychological profile, the next step was detoxification. The process for this varied by clinic, either a synthetic drug, methadone, or cold turkey, where no replacement drug is used.

Cold turkey for Miranda was a living hell. Along with the physical manifestations of detox, she battled her psychological demons. As a child of parents with abnormal brain function, their pattern initiated a course for early disaster. Her mother, a functioning alcoholic, and her father, an adrenaline junkie, had weakened her chances for normalcy. This set the stage for PTSD and drugs were her escape. Self-medication was used to quell the nightmares also caused by years of abuse at the hands of her uncle. Often times, she awoke drenched in sweat, to Sully's horror.

She never shared her secret with anyone. Until now.

Jim Martin joined Harmony House after doing internship for his PhD graduating top of his class at American University in Washington, D.C. As valedictorian, he could have written his own ticket and practiced in the capitol city. But, being a Cleveland boy, he relocated back to his hometown and picked this clinic merely because it was close to his apartment. As an avid bike rider, he refused to own a car, and as luck would have it, the clinic was ten blocks away.

This perfect specimen of a man continued to be a conundrum for his fellow workers at Harmony. Extremely reserved with a penetrating green-eyed stare, he worked diligently and efficiently. Therefore, his case load was heavy, intense and he was always assigned hardcore cases. In the anatomy of this "counseling machine," popular with both the staff and the patients, there was one little flaw.

He was an emotional wreck.

He internalized every patients' case, taking home and mentally reliving every detail of their horrible stories. He analyzed and re- analyzed and drove himself crazy until he found the perfect program for their rehabilitation.

This obsession led to his non-relationship status. All the better for his clients.

Miranda O'Sullivan broke his heart. From their earliest sessions, her story haunted him nightly.

"Do you think your mother knew?" Jim asked during a session. "I don't know and I don't care," she replied angrily.

"Did you hate her?"

"No. I just felt sorry for her." "Why?"

"She had a horrible life and drank because of it."

"So, you blame your father," he continued to peel away the layers.

"No, he provided for us, for her, but he was never there. Other than a white-water rafting trip with dad in West Virginia, I never saw him."

"And your
uncle?"

Silence.

"I don't blame my mother for taking up with the bastard." "Your Uncle Ted."

"He was one in a line of many. She actually thought I never knew, but I did most of the time. Funny thing, I kind of liked Thomas."

Jim sat up a little straighter, not recognizing this name form his files. As he flipped through his notes, she giggled.

"Thomas was the son of the gardener. She slept with both of them," she tapped on his notepad, "Write that down," she insisted.

He scribbled the name in his notes. "Back to your uncle."

She laughed uncharacteristically, "Can you imagine being molested repeatedly by your father's twin bother? There's a movie in there somewhere."

"Shall we write it and make a fortune?" he answered uncomfortably.

"It will have to be a horror story," she shook her head, "Let's just get through this."

He could see form her expression that she was reliving every moment.

"Your use of heroin…" Jim prodded.

"Is a direct result of needing to cope with my rotten childhood, blah, blah, blah."

"Yes, PTSD."

"Really? You use that term with non-military circumstances?" "Oh God, yes. You don't think your situation doesn't count as traumatic stress?"

"You got me there."

Their sessions always ended with a traditional cup of Celestial Bliss tea and quiet time. A chance for both to process the intensity of the last hour.

Weeks of this would have driven a lesser man to drink but for Jim he had a different out.

Dymphna.

His Bianchi Vertigo 105, de-stressor, was a two grand  graduation present from his parents. He had named it after an Italian saint who lived in the 7th Century and was the daughter of a pagan Irish king and a Christian wife. Murdered by her father for her refusal to marry him, she was the Patron Saint of those afflicted with neurological disorders.

As he pedaled, late into the night instead of sleeping, he processed.

"Well, Dymphna, you'd love this one," he muttered. Yes, Dr. Martin talked to his bicycle, for hours.

Who better to help the obsessed than one of their own? The only difference was that his obsession was a safe one.

After two months and with some hesitation on his part, Miranda was released into the waiting arms of her husband.

Living in a fairy tale world of his own making, Sully believed her cured.

# CHAPTER 8

*— Life Marches On — 1996-2005*

The life of a recovering addict often parallels the experience of combat troops returning home from war. To both, a misstep can trigger a mental land mine, culminating in loss of life for the soldier or using once again. Both result with a restart of the vicious cycle.

Miranda had been leading life as a wife and mother, tentatively balancing her Narcotics Anonymous meetings with home. Since being released from Harmony House, she surprisingly had no follow-ups with the facility and the meetings became her new normalcy.

An addict.

Very simply, it's a person whose existence was controlled by drugs, continually in the grip of a progressive illness which often ends in death.

If Miranda was leading the battle, Sully followed close behind, worried at every turn and without being too abrasive, he insisted on daily meetings and a kept a closer eye on her. Knowing the distance to and from meetings, he often checked her odometer.

She found out by accident while looking for her checkbook. Thinking she had left it in his desk, she found a journal he was keeping. Scribbled on the pages were his feelings on the whole process and dated mileage notes.

Two things were evident to her, he was tracking her every move and he was totally devoted to her and making their marriage work. She never told him she had found his journal, but it had created an awkwardness in their union.

Life for the household had returned to normal until a couple of years later when the landmine was triggered.

"So dad, what brings you back to the states?" she queried coolly, not having seen him in years.

"Some back tax issues I needed to deal with here," he replied non-committedly, "And some news."

Miranda's father, Harry, had returned from Europe newly married. Having been widowed for a number of years, he met a woman on a ski trip and proposed to the divorcé within just weeks.

Trigger.

"I have a new wife."

"Oh," she said

flatly.

"And we have a girl on the

way." Ka-boom.

Instantaneously, visions of years of molest-ation flooded back into her head, almost causing her to faint.

Misunderstanding her reaction, he joked, "I'm not too old to have kids."

Time for my revelation, Dad.

"Well thank God for her, your brother is dead."

"What does Ted have to do with this?" he asked, per-plexed. "Luckily nothing, that's one safe little girl."

His confusion persisted.

"Let me spell it out for you, dad. This little girl was molested by Uncle Ted for ten years while her mother drank and you skied."

He sat with a thud.

"Each year on the anniversary of my independ-ence, I celebrate," she laughed, "I celebrate the day Uncle Ted was killed by one of his own trucks. Pretty fucking ironic."

Still speechless, she mimicked the all-too-famous speech. "Free at last, I'm free at last."

She looked him dead in the

eyes. "And you wonder why

I'm an addict."

He struggled to find the right words, "I'm sorry that happened to you."

"Ancient history."

But not so ancient, for little did Miranda know Harry's revelation would initiate another downward spiral once more.

Emboldened by her father-daughter conversation, she decided Sully should also know the demons inside her were not of her own making.

On one of the few nights he was home, the stage was set for her dramatic turn. Not surprising to her, dishes went flying, a rare demonstration of temper, new to her, and gratifying. It's about time someone else was angry.

"And you lived with this for all these years?" he asked incredulously, "Did your mother know?"

"Oh, the million dollar question," she mused, "I suspect she did.

That's why she drank and ultimately killed herself, finally leaving me alone."

"I'm glad you survived," he searched for something else to say. "Some days, so am I."

The following day, knowing her mileage would be checked by Sully when he returned home, Miranda drove to Saint Anthony's Church for her NA meeting and parked the car as usual.

She boarded the 107 bus and exited the stop at Quicker Liquor. Mounting the familiar creaking stairway, she knocked tentatively on the door of Apartment 1.

A familiar face greeted her with a dazed smile. "Hello princess, welcome home."

Without the ubiquitous movie montage and the "Valley of the Dolls" theme playing the background, Miranda slipped into the abyss of addiction.

# CHAPTER 9

*— Best Performance by an Actress — 2005*

Miranda once again balanced life with Sully and Arthur, now aged 6, and a new child on the way. This was of the utmost concern due to the fact she wasn't quite sure just whose baby it was. She loved Sully, but her attraction to Luke was another addiction and too much for her to resist.

She knew premature births and low birth weight were a typical danger during pregnancy for someone on drugs, but Miranda would face none of these. Twenty-two weeks into her pregnancy, the fetus was stillborn.

Sully was anxious to add children to his family and the death of his unborn child was devastating.

She still had it all. A beautiful home, a loving husband and a beautiful child with all the perks that affluence provided, was not enough.

Because shadowing every hour of every day, was Luke and his party favors, heroin and booze. Add to this cocktail, a new ingredient, George.

An import from Brazil, George found his way to the Cleveland area as a bouncer at the Kiddy Klub, an after-hours, underage dance club serving non-alcoholic drinks. Virgin everything, except for the kids. Despite the "no booze" moniker, everything else was served here. Sex, drugs and rock"n"roll.

George worked the crowd with his suave de-
meanor and sexual prowess, having no problem with
his underage partners, both men and women. Along
with his body came his drug connections. Hot and
heroin was a deadly combination and the lack of a
moral compass added to the sense of danger. He was
ever-present and ever-popular, even when not on
duty.

Miranda had often questioned Luke about how the
two had met.

He was evasive in his answers and she imagined they
had been partners in more than smack.

Luke never admitted his bisexual nature to anyone,
especially Miranda. His years in jail and taught him
how to use sex as a bargaining tool. There, it was just
commerce. You paid for what

you got, only instead of bills, you used your body. It had nothing to do with sex.

In his mind, he wasn't gay, he was just paying for goods.

Life continued to spiral out of control with the complication of a heroin-addicted child successfully averted. Because a child born to an addicted mother can result in Neonatal Abstinence Syndrome (NAS), babies born in this condition include symptoms like irritability, seizures, stunted weight gain, excessive diarrhea and vomiting. Many times, the combination resulted in death of the child.

Miranda, not a bad person, never learned her lesson and continued on her merry way, as Billie Holiday would have described it.

Saturday night, January 29, 2005 was uncharacteristically frigid night in the city. Partying above Quicker Liquor was in full swing. Both Luke and George, along with a financial aid endowment from Miranda, had scored some high-quality H- Bomber with a purity of over 70% from The Netherlands. All three imbibed in the festivities with no one operating as the trip-sitter, the babysitter for travel down the smack highway.

Luke had decided a bottle of Grey Goose could only add to the party and hit up Miranda for some extra cash.

"Gimme a fifty, babe," Luke begged, hand extended. She waved toward her purse.

"Be right back," he said as he staggered away from the purse and toward the door.

"Oh damn, Quicker is closed," he said pounding the doorframe, "I'll go to Sal's, it's only about ten blocks away."

He closed the door.

"Hey, it's just us," slurred George as he patted the

seat next to him on the couch.

The smile has electrifying and uncharacteristic for a supposed poor boy from the streets of Brazil.

But George was not really George at all.

Fernando Gustavo, was a fugitive from the São Paulo Police for repeated aggravated sexual assault. Unbeknownst to U.S. authorities, the suave, ruggedly handsome passport holder at U.S. Customs in Houston, Texas was really "The Seaweed Rapist." This was a title bestowed by the press due to the circumstance of finding the victims on the beach half-buried in sand and seaweed.

Now Miranda had never found the allure of George particularly compelling as did countless others. She was a two-man woman who never looked for a third, albeit her distorted and twisted view of monogamy.

Yet, to George she was a conquest.

"There must be something else to drink around here," he said as he arose and rummaged through the stain and filth of the mini- kitchen. Finding a forgotten half-bottle of Jameson's whiskey, he grabbed two empty glasses and plopped it all in front of Miranda.

Dazed enough to not notice the powder he slipped into her glass; she drank the pour with abandon. The GHB had its intended effect quickly due to the combination with the heroin in her system and the booze used to wash it down.

George wasted little time with small talk since the drowsiness and dizziness began to show after only ten minutes. The charm disappeared just as quickly and a maniacal deviant emerged in his place. The ensuing rape was almost clinical, fast and efficient. Brutally evasive to Miranda's unconscious body and violent to the point of extreme, George pushed her aside and her head hit the floor with a thud.

Redressing himself, he noticed Miranda was racked with seizures.

"You bitch," he seethed as he lifted her like a sack of potatoes. He needed to get her help and to avoid discovery and detention by American authorities.

At 11:45 PM, while Luke was purchasing his Grey Goose at Sal's, George sped past in a stolen vehicle with Miranda perched on the passenger seat.

It was mid-shift at St. Vincent and things were typically quiet before the rush of the bars closing and the usual stabbings and shootings got into full-swing after 2 AM.

Dr. Patrick Edwards' time was consumed by an atypical frostbite case of a teenage boy who jumped from a bridge into the Potomac River.

Nurse Lopez stuck her head in the bay, "Our frequent flier is back in Bay 5. The cops brought him in, and he awaits your presence," she smiled, "Don't worry, he's in Siamese Friendship Bracelets, but be careful, he's a biter."

Dr. Edwards chuckled to himself at Lopez' dramatic description of handcuffs, "Siamese bracelets."

A blaring auto horn sounded outside the entrance. "What the fuck!" she habitually uttered.

"Lopez..."

"Sorry doctor, Father," she stammered, not used to his double title.

Lopez and an intern ran out the door and found an abandoned vehicle, driver door open, with an unresponsive female in the passenger seat. As the intern carried her to a gurney, Lopez ran ahead to alert Dr. Edwards.

"Forget the popsicle," indicating the boy Edwards was working on, "We have a comatose female, approximately early thirties with signs of sexual assault."

Once again, Miranda had returned home.

# CHAPTER 10

*— Rock Bottom — 2005-2010*

The patient had a torn dress, no underwear, one missing shoe and multiple bruises. Her nose was bleeding profusely and she had strong odor of alcohol on her breath, but was breathing and had a pulse. Her vital signs were 120/80, HR 86, RR 24 and the patient was then put on a Narcan drip.

After Miranda had been stabilized, she awoke and admitted only to doing heroin and some drinking.

"We'd like to do a rape kit," he suggested.

"No need to... it was just a bad fall," she mumbled.

Lopez thought to herself, "Of course it was, and when fell you tore underwear and bruised your vaginal area."

"No rape kit," she insisted.

Dr. Edwards started a search for her identity with one of the first year doctors.

"Look for the same drug-related cases with similar stats," Dr. Edwards coached, "I have a hunch we've seen this Jane Doe before."

Dr. Chad Jeremy was used to the grunt work of the E.R. and never really minded it much. He was a good Christian and knew it was just part of the job. He felt sorry for each and every patient who came through the door and that would be his downfall as a good doctor. The cases eventually became too personal and his objectivity would be lost. But he believed that God had a plan for all of us and about a year later, while eating at his favorite health- food restaurant, he was approached by a stranger with a novel idea.

"Pardon me, but I have an odd question," the stranger asked, "I assume from your scrubs, you're a doctor."

"That's correct," Chad replied, wondering to himself why that was odd.

"Do you by any chance speak Spanish?" "In fact, I do, and also Japanese."

"Perfect," said Ricardo Diaz, Telemundo talent scout.

Two weeks later, Chad Jeremy would be on his way to Mexico City as the new star in "Los Rompecorazones," a story about a young, handsome doctor from the states who falls in love with Anita, having saved her from the jaws of death after a serious car accident. Her father, the President of Mexico, had planned differently for his daughter and drama ensued. Lots of clandestine meetings and Chad would be shirtless for most of the season.

While the doctors worked on Jane Doe, he sat at the computer researching past cases in the archived files.

Miranda's insistence on not having a rape kit administered was for self-preservation. Sully would know and it would also be reported. Somewhere in her mind, she felt she could hide this incident and save her marriage. It certainly wasn't for George's sake. She knew he would be long-gone by the time she got back to Luke's apartment.

Luke himself had discovered this when he returned to the apartment just about the time Miranda was regaining consciousness in the E.R. His first clue was a lone shoe in the stairwell, secondly, the apartment door was ajar and lastly there was no trace of George or Miranda. He knew something had happened.

Ironically, it was Luke who reported Miranda as a missing person, posing as her husband.

Dr. Jeremy search through the computer records was successful and he was confident he had found the identity of their Jane Doe. It would have to wait for the next day's shift as Dr.
Edwards had gone home, and the patient had been stabilized.

"Is this Robert O'Sullivan?" the voice on the other end of the line questioned.

"It is," Sully replied distractedly as he juggled the phone with a note from the nanny that said she had taken their son to a movie.

"This is Sergeant Robbins at the 3rd Precinct and we

found your wife."

"I'm confused," he uttered as he pulled up a stool and sat at the breakfast bar, "Found my wife. Where?"

"You reported her missing yesterday? She's at St. Vincent." "What happened?"

"You'll have to check that with the hospital yourself."

Sully remembered her car was not in the garage and rushed to the hospital envisioning an accident.

"My wife was admitted?" he prodded the woman behind the window at Admitting.

"Name?"

"Miranda O'Sullivan."

"Hold on," she checked the screen and picked up the phone, "Could you page Dr. Edwards to Admitting?"

Momentarily, Dr. Edwards beckoned Sully to follow him into his office.

"Dr. Edwards," he extended his hand to Sully, "I wanted to speak with you before you see your wife. She was admitted late yesterday with a heroin overdose, alcohol poisoning and we assume a sexual assault. She refused a rape kit."

Sully sat dumbfounded, mostly at his own ignorance. He saw the signs, ignored them and blamed himself for this episode.

"As you probably realize, this is not the first time we have seen your wife in the E.R.," Dr. Edwards said as he opened the file Dr. Jeremy gave him earlier that day.

"Yes, I recognized you, but I had forgotten your name," Sully said.

"She needs to go to rehab."

"She's been to one before," he said, discouraged.

"Yes, Harmony House," he nodded, "Was there anything you can think of that might have triggered a relapse?"

Sully fell silent.

"Look, I know it might be hard, but it will be between us. If it makes you feel better, I can put on my other hat." He reached into his desk and pulled out a Roman collar.

Sully sat, staring.

"Odd, I know," he smiled, "Many people are prone to a double life and I am no exception. I became a doctor and after my wife died, I decided to follow my second passion and was ordained a Roman Catholic priest."

"They can do that?" Sully said.

"Yes, I'm called a 'Second Generation' priest."

"So, anything I say is under the Seal of Confession?" "Oh, you're Catholic?"

"Fallen away."

"Well, come back. We need you," Dr. Edwards joked. "Discussion for another day," Sully concluded the subject. "Absolutely."

He reached into his desk and pulled out a pamphlet.

"So, New Beginnings is an addiction treatment facility with full, wrap-around services." He handed it to Sully, who was hesitant to read it.

Dr. Edwards noticed Sully's reticence, "Are you ready for round two?"

"I love her, but I'm just not sure. I do have a son to think about as well."

"Her addiction is manageable, but it takes time and patience." "Something I'm running out of," Sully whispered.

# CHAPTER 11

*— New Beginnings*

Grace O'Farrell stared at the file in front of her and smiled at the small ironies in life. Staring back at her from the papers was a person she had often thought of over the last 15 years. Her "sandwich girl" from under the Veterans Memorial Bridge so many cold nights ago, was back.

Unfortunately, Miranda would join New Beginnings as a client for her own new beginning. Her treatment would be in-house and around the clock with the help of trained mental health professionals and a full nursing staff. They worked to build patterns for her life that should preserve sustainable sobriety. Due to her track record, she would be enrolled for a 90-day stay with little contact to life outside of the facility. She would participate in support group meetings, work one-on-one with her counselor and each step of her treatment would be molded for her by her team.

Life inside the center was a controlled environment which afforded no chance to relapse. Obviously, once the client left the facility, the real work started.

A soft knock on the door preceded its opening as Miranda stepped into the room. The recognition was instantaneous.

"I know you," smiled Miranda, relieved.

"And I you, my sweet friend," Grace broke protocol and embraced her.

Although the ensuing three months were not easy for Miranda, she was a model client. She participated fully in her regime, even opting for an added month, during which she began bridging her life inside New Beginnings with her life at home.

Grace recognized the fragility of this transition for Miranda would not be easy and her gut feeling was that New Beginnings would ultimately fail her. She felt bad about the nagging feeling in her gut, but years of experience had given her a keen sense of those who could and couldn't stick with it.

Miranda returned home to a more reserved Sully and a teenaged Arthur. The feeling that she was being watched by her husband was hard to shake and made for an uncomfortable day- to-day routine.

"The transition is hard for me," she spoke softly over breakfast. "I know... it's hard for both of us," Sully replied, "But I'm not going anywhere."

She reached across the table and touched his hand, "Thank you."

Part of the outreach of New Beginnings included a check-in every 90 days. Grace made sure she was the one to personally monitor Miranda's case.

"Maybe you should get a little job, not for the money but merely to give back," Grace suggested.

"Well, Sully has the restaurants and Arthur and I..." "Are not close?"

"Not yet."

Grace added, "Well, he's a teenager." Miranda nodded in agreement. "Have you heard from your father?"

"Thank God, no. He's out there living his life far away from mine."

They quietly finished their tea and Grace breathed a sigh of relief that for the moment, everything seemed stable. Maybe for once that gut feeling was wrong.

In 2008, Miranda took Arthur to the movies to see "The Boy in the Striped Pajamas." It has become a welcomed outing for mother and son to have lunch and see a film together. Arthur had warmed up to his mother in her new sober role and she had realized the distance between them was her own fault.

Heroin does that to families.

On their return home, there was a letter waiting in the mail from an overseas address. It was from her father's new wife and contained a separate letter he had written in the event of his death.

There are several warning signs that an addict is about to relapse. Although relapse is too often common, it doesn't usually occur without warning. Triggers are just that, a firing that leads an addict to beat a path back to their favorite addiction. Leaving behind a devoted family, the addict is susceptible to certain places, events or psychiatric issues.

Miranda's issue, a letter from your dead father telling you he suspected all along that you were being molested by his brother, but being a coward, he didn't know how to deal with it.

As she read through the letter from the new wife, she realized that Harry was up to his old tricks of traveling instead of dealing with life. He had left his new wife and baby for thrill challenge number blah, blah, blah and died in an avalanche in Nepal while at Base Camp 4.

Miranda didn't know why his death affected her so much, considering he was never around for her. A discovery like this might even push a normal person over the edge, but Miranda was anything but normal and over the edge she plummeted.

In the year 2010, Miranda would again make a midnight visit to her second home, St. Vincent.

# CHAPTER 12

*— Repair, Restore & Renew — 2011*

189 Elm Street, a well-kept, non-descript professional environment was the result of a think-tank run by several top physicians in greater Cleveland. Now headed up by Dr. Brianna Benton who was educated at the University of Oxford Medical School in England, it was to be Miranda's next home.

Dr. Edwards and Sully had petitioned 189 to take on Miranda's case after an initial interview, which did not go well. The staff seemed hesitant to take on a client who had previously been unsuccessful with several rehabilitation centers.

"This is the perfect client for us," Dr. Benton calmly insisted to her team, "Our approach is much different than those she has previously attended."

At four foot ten, Dr. Brianna Benton was a force to be reckoned with, a constant presence at board meetings, petitioning for her patients.

She seldom took 'no' for an answer. She felt Mrs. O'Sullivan was a perfect challenge for 189 Elm and she could also afford the treatment, which was not inexpensive. Highly personalized with a staff to client ratio unheard of in the practice, money was often dividing line between those who needed them and those who could afford it.

Robert O'Sullivan and Dr. Edwards from St. Vincent

were out of options, and the bottom-line was Dr. Benton knew their approach could help. Often time her board forgot who was the boss and who had invested her life to this clinic.

Often times at the expense of her own family.

Miranda O'Sullivan was admitted as an out-patient on a rainy Monday morning. Although many feel rain is an ominous sign, Dr. Benton welcomed it. To her, rain was symbolic of cleansing and washing away, initiating new growth.

A thorough neuropsychiatric evaluation consisting of an exhausting questionnaire was administered and filled out by both Miranda and her husband.

"So many questions," Miranda sighed under her breath to Sully. "Look, Miranda, we want it to work," he assured her.

"Aren't you sick of me
yet?" "Not even close,"
he beamed.

He realized a big part of the problem was him. He traveled too much and secretly he had feared the time away from home was reminiscent of her father. He immediately sold the King Arthur location in D.C. at a huge profit and was now in the process of interviewing a handful of top restaurant managers to run the Cleveland location for him.

The extensive questionnaire was a tool for the team to assess a panoramic view of her behaviors, her lengthy medical history, past rehabilitation centers and hospital admissions. The team then performed a functional triad assessment, a Brain SPECT exam, a QEEG test, a Genomind test and an Ondamed energetic evaluation.

Dr. Benton scheduled a consultation with Mr. & Mrs. O'Sullivan.

"Fourteen percent of women with a history of childhood sexual abuse have some degree of drug dependency," Dr. Benton noted.

She pointed to the plaques on the walls around her.

"These academic credentials look beautiful up on the wall and do nothing but gather dust," she joked, "As therapists, we also need years of experience to deal with problems such as yours. But you, too, have to trust your instincts. After this visit, if we don't feel right for you, let us know and we will place you elsewhere. This is like a marriage."

Following the initial interview, Dr. Benton concluded that Miranda was bipolar and had PTSD from her enormous sexual and psychological trauma. Further medical tests indicated Lyme Disease, a bacterial infection from a tick bite. Through a process of elimination, they assumed Miranda was bitten during a water rafting trip with father in West Virginia. To complete the trifecta, she also had mercury poisoning apparently from her mother, who was full of mercury amalgams passed on in utero. Mercury poisoning and Lyme Disease have been previously associated with bipolar disorder.

Dr. Benton began a treatment of her bipolar disorder and PTSD, along with supplements Miranda needs to mimic what the opiates and alcohol she craved. Along with neurofeedback to retrain her brain to perform better, she also began behavioral therapy with

EMDR (Eye Movement Desensitization and Reprocessing therapy) to desensitize her from prior trauma.

A six month program was added to the regime for mercury detoxification along with weekly I.V. and daily at home ozone insufflations to clear her system from the Lyme Disease bacteria. The ozone also eliminated Hepatitis C that Miranda had from sharing needles with her jailed boyfriend, Luke, and HIV that she contracted from George.

After six months of treatment, Miranda was left with medication for her Bipolar disorder and ongoing online telemedicine therapy.
There was no trace of Lyme or the other viruses plaguing her health.

Life in the O'Sullivan house was not perfect, but due to the partnership with 189 Elm and Dr. Benton, it seemed for the first time as though she was on the road to recovery. Miranda was working her program and Sully was staying closer to home. They were even expecting a new child.

# EPILOGUE

While Miranda O'Sullivan is a fictional character and her story has a happy ending, sadly our current healthcare system in the United States does not.

The crises in both the health care and criminal justice systems run parallel. The underlying problem is the same, poorly functioning brains that cause people to make poor choices that lead them into legal trouble, health trouble or both.

The solution: the integration of criminal justice science with neuropsychiatry.

Maybe convicted felons should be offered the choice of neuropsychiatric assessment and pending rehabilitation, or a month in jail. They would decide which would better modify their behavior. There are a lot of if's and maybe's, but only with integration of politics, business (i.e. money) and medical science will we move forward to a better state.

Currently, we have physicians and nurses stampeding out of medicine due to the bullying of third-party payers inflicted upon the medical field and penalties from rules made years now concerning technologies that do not exist yet. It's a non-solution because it's not targeting the problem. Why spend money on a system that is not delivering health care, but just delivering us from death. In other words, it's not making us healthy, it's just keeping us alive, a criminal law system that does not deter crime, because substance abuse is not a crime it is an illness. Illnesses do not go away with a $120/day time out at a not so comfy hotel.

The result is an enormous population of unhealthy, chronically ill patients that never get healed and keep coming back to the hospital or to the jails. This costs us an alarming $120 billion dollars as of 2010.

Mirroring this is the enormous population of criminals caught in a vicious cycle. Not being rehabbed, they continue to return to jail, continue to get released and continue to commit crimes all over again.

Repetitious and costly.

This is a global issue, although some countries deal with the issue better than others. It's about the survival of the human race as we know it.

To err is human and to be egocentric is, as well. Sadly, the world is often filled with criminals in power, resulting in man's inhumanity to man.

The most recent assault occurred in Sierra Leone where Dr. Rowen and staff brought ozone to the country and as soon as the government found out the treatment was effective, they were expelled.

Why?

Because the country gets money from international aid organizations for their health crisis, so if the crisis is cured, they lose the money.

The human paradox.

Just as Miranda continued to take responsibility of her health, that's all we can strive to do too.

In good health,

Dr. Liam Alexander Briones

# APPENDIX

**Resources for substance abuse treatment**:

1)         Substance Abuse and Mental Health Services Administration. http://www.samhsa.gov/

2) For a list of local free or low cost addiction centers visit:____http://www.freeaddictioncenters.com/city/oh-cleveland

3) Dr Amen Clinics: http://www.amenclinics.com/locations/

4)         Medical Rejuvenation Institute : Heal your brain. Medicalrejuvenationinstitute.com-currently not accepting new patients. Consultations to health care providers and institutions available upon request.

**References**:

1) Correctional Populations in the United States, 2013. Bulletin US department of Justice. December 2014, NCJ 248479

2) Criminal Victimization, 2009. Bulletin US dept of Justice. October 2010, NCJ 231327

3) Henrichson and Delaney. The Price of Prisons: What incarceration Costs Taxpayers. 2012. Vera Institute of Justice. www.Vera.org

4) Amen, Daniel MD. It's time to Stop Flying Blind: How not looking at the Brain Leads to Missed Diagnoses, Failed Treatments, and Dangerous Behaviors. Alternative therapies. Mar/ Apr 2013. Vol 19. No. 2. –Amen-The Brain, Diagnoses, Treatments and Behaviors.

# APPENDIX 2:

*Real life perspectives.*

**ADAM II 2013 Report**.
Arrestee Drug Abuse and monitoring program. Office of National . Drug control Policy. Executive Office of the President. Positive urine drug test in arrested males.

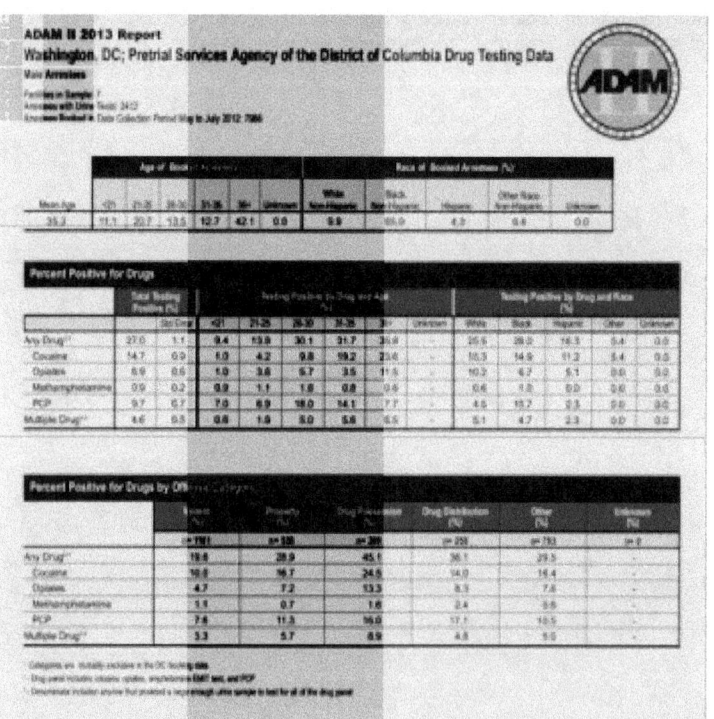

Perhaps another way to look at this data is about a quarter of arrestees the charge was drug possession or drug distribution with cocaine and PCP being the most frequently found. It would be interesting to know the financial impact of turning drug possession into a mental illness and drug distribution into a taxable trade. In the mean time, every week a drug user dies or almost dies from overdoses of heroin and other opiates at our emergency departments. The ones that survive come in with horrible infections almost losing their limbs from the swelling that cuts their circulation and bacteria that destroys their body. Those who come trying to get the limited help we can offer, tell us that they are starving for drug rehab programs, that the rehabs programs they go to just help temporarily and access is seriously limited, they feel helpless and trapped, their lives are miserable and they do not want to do drugs, but they can't stop on their own. Of course, they can't...drugs fulfill a chemical imbalance need they have but they are self-medicating with readily available choices...

Last week the 22 year old driver of a vehicle running away from the police after a suboxone party died instantly upon hitting a telephone pole, his 21 year old girlfriend was flown from the scene in critical condition and his best friend unrestrained front seat passenger, broke his neck flying out the broken windshield, the battery of the car landed on his belly...there were ruptured intestines as well...he was alive and was flown to the nearest trauma center as well...

Drug use is a crime; drug trade is a crime, yet they continue...a paradigm shift is needed from the political, social and medical standpoint.

Let's dream to see true correction of inmates and true rehabilitation of substance abusers.

In good health,
Dr. Briones MD, MBA.